Designated England's first 'Area of Outstanding Natural Beauty', The Q
are a joy to behold at any time of the year.

Comprising wind-swept heather and gorse moors,
to secluded wooded combes (the haunt of the wild red
with interesting old villages and welcoming pubs scattered abou
the Quantock Hills are without question 'a treasure of English Delights'.

This little pocket book aims to capture something of their 'spirit' in beautiful photographs taken by professional photographer Paul Savage.

The Quantock Year

A CIP record for this publication is available from the British Library ISBN 9781916068711

Spring Babies

Springtime

West Somerset Railway

7820

'...walks extend for miles over the hilltops, the great beauty of which is their wild simplicity.'
Dorothy Wordsworth
1771 – 1855

Wild flower meadow above Stogumber

Looking over Cothelstone Park towards the Blackdowns

Roaming free

Quantock Ponies

The wild red deer

Watchet Harbour

BALMORAL

Hawkridge Reservoir

Kilve Beach

Evening light

Autumn in Bincombe

Home for Christmas

Ponies in Winter

Crowcombe Combe

Ploughing Match above East Combe

Crowcombe Park to Minehead

Shervage Woods